942.084

SIR HENRY COOPER HIGH SCHOOL
LIBRARY

Finding Out About
LIFE IN BRITAIN IN WORLD WAR II

Madeline Jones

Batsford Academic and Educational Ltd *London*

Contents

9333

SIR HENRY COOPER HIGH SCHOOL LIBRARY

Introduction	3
Useful Sources	4
The Coming of War	6
New Sights and Sounds	8
The First Evacuees	10
Invasion Threat, 1940	12
The "Blitz"	14
Escape from The Bombs	16
School Life	18
University Life	20
Service Life	22
War Work	24
Helping the War-Effort	26
Censorship and Propaganda	28
Food	30
Clothes	32
Separated Families	34
Allies in Britain	36
Travel in War-Time	38
1944: "D Day" and Flying-Bombs	40
Amusements and Celebration	42
Date List	44
Difficult Words	45
Places to Visit	46
Map	47
Book List	47
Index	48

© Madeline Jones 1983
First published 1983
Second impression 1984

All rights reserved. No part of this publication may be reproduced, in any form or by any means, without permission from the Publisher

Typeset by Tek-Art Ltd, Kent
and printed in Great Britain by
R.J. Acford
Chichester, Sussex
for the publishers
Batsford Academic and Educational
an imprint of B.T. Batsford Ltd,
4 Fitzhardinge Street
London W1H 0AH

ISBN 0 7134 3665 4

ACKNOWLEDGMENTS

The Author and Publishers would like to thank the following for their kind permission to reproduce the illustrations in this book: BBC Hulton Picture Library, page 3; Mrs M. Clements, pages 8, 10, 11; Miss M. Cooke, pages 5, 22; Imperial War Museum, pages 6, 23, 24, 39 (left); Mrs H.M. Jones, pages 18, 35; Mansell Collection Ltd, cover photo, left; Watford Museum, page 46; H. Weissenborn, the linocuts on pages 14 and 16. The map on page 47 was drawn by Rudolph Britto. The photographs on pages 4 and 12 are copyright of the Author.

Thanks are also due for permission to use the following extracts: the table on page 34, with permission of the Controller of Her Majesty's Stationery Office; "War Poet", from *The Collected Poems of Sidney Keyes* (ed. Michael Meyer), with permission of Routledge & Kegan Paul Ltd; extracts from Alun Lewis, "All Day It Has Rained" from *Raiders Dawn*, and "Lance Jack" from *Last Inspection & Other Stories*, with permission of George Allen & Unwin Ltd; and from William Plomer, "Ah, that ingenious Ministry of Food" from *The Autobiography of William Plomer*, with permission of The Estate of William Plomer and Jonathan Cape Ltd.

Introduction

Britain went to war against Nazi Germany in September 1939 when Hitler invaded Poland. The British had promised to help the Poles, Germany refused to withdraw her troops and war followed.

The war lasted for six years, until August 1945. In 1941 it became a "world war", with Russia and America fighting as Britain's allies and Japan joining Germany as the enemy. The reasons why all these countries fought each other are interesting to find out about: so is the actual fighting that took place in Europe, Africa and the Far East. This book, however, aims to help you to discover more about wartime life on your own doorstep. You will probably have heard and read something about the hardships of the time: you may have seen old newsreels on television as well as plays and films with a war-time background. You will want to check ideas about the war that you already have against the details you can dig out from accounts written at the time. In this book you will find samples of the sort of material you can use; you may well discover more sources of information for yourselves.

You will find evidence of danger and anxiety. In a church magazine produced in Kent in May 1940 the Rector started his message:

> The magazine is published late this month, because it has seemed impossible to write anything that would not be out of date before this . . . could be in your hands. As I write now it is hard to make any plans that may not need to be revised by national emergency . . .

If you look at pages 12-13, or at the Date List on page 44, you will discover what "emergency" the Rector feared.

Every part of the country, and every family in it, rich or poor, was affected by the war. Civilian casualties were high (60,000 killed) and King George VI created a new civilian medal for acts of great bravery — the George Cross "which will rank next to the Victoria Cross . . .". Damage was widespread.

> Much of Clydebank presents a scene of devastation in which parts of the town have been so obliterated that they already look like a backyard, and will soon look like a field or a wood . . .

wrote the poet Stephen Spender in 1945,

Everyone was affected by the war. Here King George VI and Princess Elizabeth (our present Queen) are practising working a stirrup pump. These pumps were used to put out small fires caused by incendiary bombs.

Useful Sources

after a visit to Scotland. Individuals took on all kinds of extra work. A Shropshire railwayman's daughter remembers her father's life in these "heavy years" — "long hours at work — sometimes during the night delivering supplies to Red Cross centres — many nights out on Home Guard manoeuvres" — and coming home to a house crowded with evacuee nieces expecting to be played with.

Some older people, looking back at war-time life, still remember the good side more clearly than the bad. People had to mix with each other, to work together and to help each other. Rich and poor discovered more about each other. Some young men from prosperous families found themselves sent to work in the coal-mines as "Bevin Boys", instead of into the armed forces. One young reporter was soon writing back from Doncaster to his newspaper in the South East:

> What people in non-mining parts of the country forget is that a collier's life is one of the hardest there is ...

It is not surprising that support for social reforms — better education, better health-care, better housing — grew. Even before the war ended, the 1944 Education Act tried to improve the quality of state schools and the Beveridge Report put forward plans for better social security, including a National Health Service. People hoped that life "after the war" would be better for everybody than it had been before. You might like to find out for yourselves sometime whether or not they were disappointed.

1 PEOPLE TO ASK

a) *Librarians* Go to your Public Library. The Librarian in charge of the Reference Library, or of the Local History section if there is one, will be able to tell you what material the Library has on life in the Second World War. Some libraries have their own special collections of local photographs, accounts of war-time experiences, etc.

b) *Teachers* Your own teachers may have family photographs or papers to show you. Your Headmaster or Headmistress will know whether there are any war-time written records, like log-books, in your school.

c) *Older relatives and friends* Ask older people if they can remember the war, or if they have kept any documents or mementoes. Perhaps you can collect material for a display in school. Try to tape or write down interesting war-time memories (remember, though, that people may not remember every detail exactly: sometimes you can check dates and other facts by looking at written records like old newspaper accounts).

2 VISUAL MATERIALS

a) *Buildings, memorials, inscriptions* Some towns have preserved parts of bombed buildings (like the old Coventry Cathedral) or

A pill-box, Hayling Island, Hampshire.

labelled new buildings replacing those destroyed by enemy action (in London, the new Barbican centre was developed on a bomb-site). Are there any remains of old air-raid shelters in your area? or a "pill-box"? War-memorials list those killed in the 1939-45 war, as well as in the 1914-18 war. (At Victoria Station in London, you can find a good example of a memorial to a special group — in this case, members of the Southern Railway.)

b) *Maps and pictures* Your local Library or Town Hall may have maps showing bomb-damage in your area. Look for old family photographs, and for library-collections. Artists drew and painted war-time scenes: a special group of "war-artists" were employed by the government to record important events and details of everyday life. Many of their works are in the Imperial War Museum in London, and your local Library will probably have reproductions of some famous examples like Henry Moore's "Shelter drawings".

c) *Objects* Local museums sometimes have a war-time display (you can see an example on page 46). If you visit London, the London Museum has excellent mock-ups of air-raid shelters and a display of things like ration books. The Imperial War Museum also has a section on the Home Front 1939-45.

3 WRITTEN SOURCES

a) *Newspapers and magazines* Many libraries have copies of local newspapers going back to 1939-45, as well as old church magazines which provide useful information.

b) *Council minutes* Records of war-time council meetings make very interesting reading. You can imagine how busy local councils were. Try your Library first for old copies — if this fails, write to the Town or County Hall.

c) *Hansard* This detailed record of debates in Parliament gives much useful information.

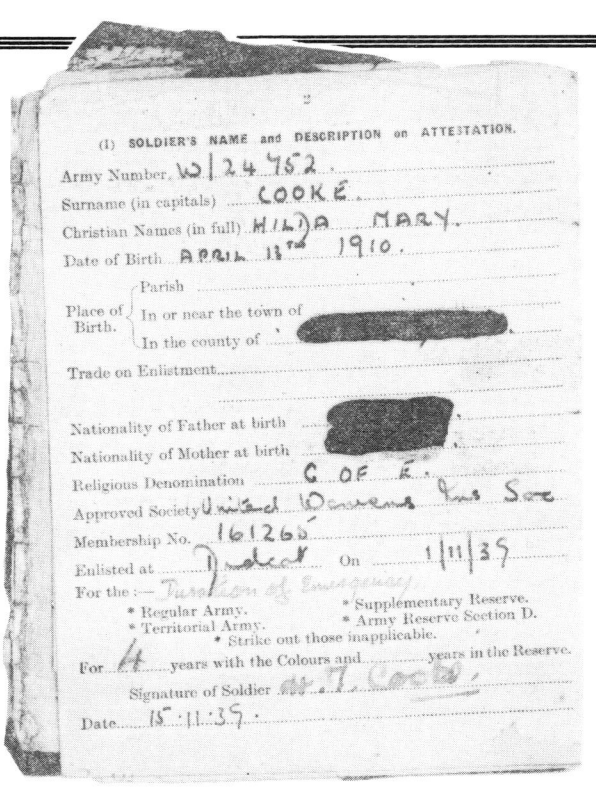

Some people still have war-time documents, like this A.T.S. Service Book.

Large libraries keep copies; ask your Librarian.

d) *Memoirs, letters, diaries* Your Library may have collected some local people's memories. Your own family may have kept old letters or even a war-time diary.

e) *War-time documents* Everyone had ration books and identity cards: you can see examples in museums, but has anyone you know kept theirs?

f) *Books* As well as accounts of war-time experiences produced at the time, many books have since been written about the war. Your Librarian will help you to find reference books (for example, you can find details about air-raids on different parts of Britain in *The Defence of the United Kingdom* by Basil Collier — one of the many volumes of the official *History of the Second World War*). There is a list of some especially useful books on page 47.

The Coming of War

Britain declared war on Germany on 3 September 1939, but preparations began well before the actual declaration. There had nearly been a war in 1938, and a lot of plans had been made then, including one to evacuate town children to the country. The first children were moved out of big cities on 1 September 1939, many of them travelling in school groups with their teachers.

This was soon to be a familiar sight all over Britain: young servicemen arriving at camp carrying their kitbags. Military service was compulsory for men between 19 and 41. (Later, conscription was extended to boys of 18 and to women.)

The rounded huts in war-artist Alan Sorrell's picture of an R.A.F. station are called Nissen huts. At old camp-sites you can still find large concrete rectangles on which huts like these once stood.

PRECAUTIONS AT THE LONDON ZOO

Julian Huxley, in charge of the London Zoo, faced the problem of what might happen if bombs fell on the animal and reptile houses:

> The first thing I did... was to see that the black widow spiders and the poisonous snakes were killed, sad though it was, for some of the snakes were very rare as well as beautiful. I closed the aquarium and had its tanks emptied; and arranged that the elephants, who might well have run amok if frightened by the expected bombing (elephants are very nervous creatures) be moved to Whipsnade. I had previously set up an air-raid squad of keepers allowed... to carry rifles, to be on guard during the night to deal with bombs and... to shoot any dangerous animals that might escape.   (Julian Huxley, *Memories*)

PREPARATIONS IN KENT AND LONDON

Harold Nicolson, an M.P., travelled to London from his home in Kent on 1 September 1939. He wrote in his diary:

> Motor up . . . to London. There are few signs of any undue activity beyond a few khaki figures at Staplehurst and some schoolboys filling sandbags at Maidstone. When we get near London we see a row of balloons hanging like black spots in the air.
> Go down to the House of Commons at 5.30. They have already darkened the building and lowered the lights . . .
> I dine at the Beefsteak [Club] . . . . When I leave the Club, I am startled to find a perfectly black city. Nothing could be more dramatic or give one more of a shock than to leave the familiar Beefsteak and to find outside not the glitter of all the sky-signs, but a pall of black velvet.

Try to find out what sandbags were used for — and balloons (these were special "barrage balloons").

WAR IS DECLARED

At 11 o'clock on 3 September 1939, Neville Chamberlain, the Prime Minister, told the British people that they were at war with Germany. You will find that older people usually remember listening to this broadcast, even if they were young children at the time.

Marjorie Clements, the wife of a Gravesend teacher, was already on her way to Norfolk with a group of evacuees when she heard about the declaration of war:

> . . . the whole of the three schools were transported to the Royal Terrace Pier, Gravesend, and embarked on the S.S.

WHAT WAR MEANT

Harold Macmillan, who had fought in the 1914-18 war, later remembered how he had felt on the first day of this new war:

> As I walked back from the House of Commons on that afternoon, 3rd September, I thought of my son. He was now eighteen years old, and an undergraduate [student] at Oxford, as I had been twenty-five years before. He would go to the war. Would he come back? . . . (Harold Macmillan, *The Blast of War*)

Ask your older relations and friends what they can remember about 3 September 1939.

> Royal Daffodil a pleasure paddle steamer . . . . The ship got underway . . . heading for Great Yarmouth. There were plenty of organised games, amusements, and competitions to keep the children's minds away from the hazards and the sense of loneliness which many of them must have been feeling . . . . My husband was actually up on the bridge with the captain when war was declared at 11 a.m. (He was supervising competitions from there — the prizes being bars of chocolate!) The message came through to the captain and immediately the escort planes — which had been flying at a discreet distance — closed in on the ship . . .

You can read more about these evacuees on pages 10-13.

New Sights and Sounds

Of all the new war-time sounds, the most important was the air-raid warning — a wailing siren ("All Clear" was a long, steady note). Buildings and streets had to be "blacked out" so that enemy bombers could not spot any lights. Like Harold Nicolson (see page 7), many people found the total darkness a great shock. You can imagine, too, what a nuisance it was to cover up all the windows of your house or flat.

THE FIRST AIR-RAID WARNING

Duff Cooper was walking to the House of Commons on 3 September with some of his fellow M.P.s when

> ... we heard strange sounds and said, laughing, that it sounded like an air-raid warning, which indeed it proved to be. We walked on towards the House of Commons ... Derek said, 'We're walking pretty fast, aren't we?' which we were. When we arrived there we were directed to a room opposite the downstair smoking-room, which was full of an odd mixture of people — servants, typists and the Speaker. We didn't stay there long but wandered out on the terrace, where we watched the balloons go up, which they did with great speed. It was a beautiful morning. The House met at twelve as arranged and the All Clear went during Prayers ... (Duff Cooper, *Old Men Forget*)

If this account had no date, what details might tell you that a day very early in the war was being described?

◀ *Ships wrecked by mines were washed up on beaches. Sometimes mines were washed up too. Marjorie Clements, helping to look after these evacuees in Norfolk, remembers "a coastguard ... running along the top of the cliff, gesticulating madly — for he had just seen one of our bigger boys sitting astride one of these mines ... washed in by the tide".*

You may have seen an old (and harmless) mine used as a collecting box. There is one in Alfriston, East Sussex, with an inscription telling how it was washed up the River Cuckmere as far as the village.

PROTECTION FOR LOCAL COMMUNITIES

Families made their own houses as safe as possible. Shelters were built and trenches dug for use in air-raids. Members of the Air Raid Wardens' Service (A.R.P.) were trained to help in emergencies. (They also enforced the black-out regulations, and jokes were soon being made about their cries of "Put out that light".) The writer of "Rotherhithe News" in the parish magazine for Chislehurst, Kent, reported on the strange sights in his area by October 1939:

> Many of our little houses are sandbagged, and their windows decorated with festoons of gummed paper. There are long and good trenches behind the Church....
> Most of the elder Scouts are doing A.R.P. messenger work, and are very impressive in tin hats.

Can you work out the reason why people put gummed paper (or sometimes gummed net) onto the glass in their windows? (Think what happens to glass if there is an explosion.)

WAR-TIME ADVERTISEMENTS

New-style advertisements swiftly appeared in newspapers, like these from the *Beckenham and Penge Advertiser*:

> Wylie & Berlyn Ltd.
> 6, Bywood Avenue, Croydon
> AIR RAID SHELTERS
> AND
> ALL MATERIALS FOR A.R.P.
> (7 September 1939)
>
> ---
>
> Owing to the terrific increase in prices we can only offer our present stock at the old prices
> THE WISE HOUSEWIFE SHOULD PURCHASE NOW
>
> We have a stock of
> BLACK CURTAIN MATERIAL
> E.S. Richer & Co.
> (21 September 1939)

What would the black material be needed for?

> KENNARDS OF CROYDON
> DON'T WORRY
> DON'T let this present state of emergency get you.
> DON'T stay at home, carry on as usual.
> DON'T forget that shopping has to be done, and that Kennards are ready to assist you in every direction.
> DON'T mope, spend a day at Croydon and visit Kennards.
> DON'T think that Croydon is unsafe to shop in during the day ...
> (7 September 1939)

What effect did this big store fear that the war might have on its customers?

The First Evacuees

Plans had been made by the British government to send children from the big cities (which were most likely to be bombed) to stay with families in the country. During the first three days of September 1939, nearly 1½ million people (mostly children, but some mothers and some teachers too) were evacuated in this way. Some evacuees settled in happily, but others soon returned home, especially as, in the early months of the war, there were in fact very few air-raids. (When the raids did begin in 1940, a second big evacuation took place.)

EVACUEES IN NORFOLK

Many children were evacuated with schoolfriends and teachers, like those from the Whitehill Schools in Gravesend who were looked after by Marjorie Clements and her school-teacher husband (see page 7). Mrs Clements' account shows the difficulties faced both by the evacuees and by the communities which received them.

The first night was spent in Great Yarmouth, Norfolk with children and staff all distributed amongst the local schools .... They slept — if sleep came to any — on straw mattresses .... I remember my husband telling me that he had just got his room settled down for the night, older brothers and sisters helping to look after the small members of their families, when the sirens went! All had to get up, hastily put some clothes on again — collect their gas masks etc. and make for shelter. It was not a very long 'Alert' — and the 'All Clear' soon sounded — and back they all trooped in the darkness of a strange building to find their rooms and mattresses again. At last — all settled once again — and, 'Please, Sir, my little brother wants to go to the toilet!' Down four flights of stairs — across an open playground — and back again!! Oh, well!!

... a very large majority of the Whitehill Schools eventually arrived at Mundesley-on-Sea ... a very pretty Norfolk sea-side village with a widely scattered population of some 1,000 persons — two or three pubs — some small shops ... a few reasonable sized private Guest Houses — one small hotel — and the rest in very small houses and cottages .... Imagine a village of this size and description suddenly having about three hundred children of all ages — plus teachers and helpers — suddenly dumped on its doorstep.

Practically every home in the village had to have at least one or two children .... Most of the children settled down and enjoyed every minute of their sea-side 'holiday' — but, obviously, there were some who were home-sick ...

PROBLEMS TO BE SOLVED

One big problem for children who came from poor homes was that they did not have enough warm clothes. This was made worse by the fact that the first winter of the war was a very cold one. Also, town clothes were not suitable for country life. Here is a letter to Chislehurst Mothers' Union, Kent, from Bathford Vicarage, Somerset:

> 19th October, 1939
>
> Dear Members,
>   I am writing... to thank you for the splendid parcel of clothes which you have sent for the evacuated children in this Village... nearly all the money collected in the Village has been exhausted in buying shoes and material for thick coats and dresses which are being made up by experienced volunteers.

You may be able to find out about evacuees going from, or into, your own area: try the local Library for copies of old newspapers, and ask older people what they can remember.

> We have now about 50 unaccompanied children between the ages of 6-14 and 14 mothers and little children. The unaccompanied children are those we have had to clothe as many arrived from very poor homes in Poplar [London] with their one set of clothing in rags and shoes in holes ...

A Ministry of Health Circular, 1939 reported:

> It has to be recognised that in the matter of boots and clothes the needs of children in the country are different from those of children in towns. In addition to warm clothing, the provision of some form of mackintosh, preferably a cape with a hood, and of stout laced shoes or boots, or alternatively, Wellington boots, is important.

Are the evacuees in the picture wearing warm, suitable clothes?

Children from the Gravesend group in Norfolk, in the bad winter of 1939-40.

Everyone tried to give the evacuees a good Christmas. Here the Gravesend children are at a party. Look closely at their faces. Why do you think some are not as cheerful as people usually are at a Christmas party?

Invasion Threat, 1940

In May 1940, the Germans occupied Belgium and Holland and by 22 June they had defeated France too. Britain expected to be invaded next. Great preparations were made to prevent German troops from landing, as well as plans to resist them if they did manage to land. Luckily, most of the British troops in Europe were safely brought home from Dunkirk by early June. Then in August and September the R.A.F. beat off the German Air Force in the "Battle of Britain" and Hitler decided not to risk an invasion after all.

THE "HOME GUARD"

On 14 May 1940, Anthony Eden, the Secretary of State for War, broadcast an appeal for volunteers to become part-time soldiers to help defend the country against a German invasion.

> We want large numbers of ... men ... between the ages of seventeen and sixty-five .... The name of the new Force ... will be 'The Local Defence Volunteers' .... You will not be paid, but you will receive a uniform and will be armed .... In order to volunteer, what you have to do is to give in your name at your local police station ...

There are still plenty of reminders of the "Battle of Britain", like this Hurricane fighter at Biggin Hill airfield in Kent. Was there a war-time airfield in your area? Remember, it may now be used for something else. Spitfires and Hurricanes flew from Acklington in Northumberland in 1940. Today the old airfield is an open prison.

The response was tremendous: Leeds alone raised 3 battalions and 10,000 men volunteered in the county of Kent within 24 hours of Eden's speech. There were so many volunteers that it was months before they could all "receive a uniform and . . . be armed".

The name of the force, however, was soon changed:

26.VI.40.
Prime Minister to Secretary of State for War
I don't think much of the name 'Local Defence Volunteers' for your very large new force. The word 'local' is uninspiring. Herbert Morrison suggested to me today the title 'Civic Guard', but I think 'Home Guard' would be better . . . (Winston Churchill, *The Second World War*, vol. 2)

Winston Churchill was now Prime Minister: do you think he was right about "Home Guard" being a more inspiring name — and if so, why?

PEOPLE ON THE MOVE AGAIN

If the Germans came, they were most likely to land in East Anglia or on the South Coast. People from those areas were therefore encouraged to leave. This meant another move for Mr & Mrs Clements and the Gravesend evacuees:

. . . at six o'clock in the morning of 4th June [1940] we gathered outside the Coronation Hall — our sixty children with, I think, about four staff and some official helpers. All the foster-parents — who, by this time, had become very attached to their individual children — and so many of the other people of Mundesley-on-Sea . . . had come to wish us God-speed. The vicar was there to hold a little service . . . and

TAKING PRECAUTIONS

4th July 1940.
Prime Minister to General Ismay
What is being done to encourage and assist the people living in threatened sea-ports to make suitable shelters for themselves in which they could remain during an invasion?
. . . Officers or representatives of the local authority should go round explaining to families that if they decide not to leave in accordance with our general advice, they should remain in the cellars, and arrangements should be made to prop up the building overhead. They should be assisted in this both with advice and materials. Their gas-masks should be inspected . . . (Basil Collier, *History of the Second World War: The Defence of the United Kingdom*)

Churchill thought these offers of help might encourage people to leave! Do you agree? Why did the government want civilians out of the way?

the hymn "God be with you till we meet again" was sung . . .

We climbed into the two buses which were there to take us to join our special train at North Walsham, a matter of five miles away — but during that five miles we were stopped by armed soldiers on two occasions to check that our papers and identity cards were in order! Thus was the state of tension at that time . . .

The children, after "a journey which took many, many hours", eventually arrived in Leek in North Staffordshire. (If you look at a map of England you will see why Staffordshire was thought safer than Norfolk.)

The "Blitz"

Large-scale bombing of British towns (which the British called the "Blitz") began with night attacks on London in September 1940. The worst raids ended with an attack on Birmingham on 16 May 1941. Much damage was caused, and there were many casualties (about 30,000 people were killed). When raids continued night after night, people became exhausted. With over 3½ million houses damaged or destroyed, many were left homeless. In spite of all the danger, however, most people managed to "carry on", even though they were often frightened and extremely uncomfortable.

Do you recognize the church in this lino-cut picture by Helmuth Weissenborn of bomb-damaged London? Why do you think the artist has chosen to show the great Dome still standing behind the ruins? (Helmuth Weissenborn himself was a German refugee who had left Germany for Britain in 1938 after criticizing the Nazis.)

DISTURBED NIGHTS IN LONDON

Thomas Jones lived in central London, which was badly affected by the bombing. On 13 September 1940 he wrote to a friend:

> . . . the last two nights I have slept on a couch in the steward's room in the basement. The telephonist was bombed in a shelter last night; the water main burst and flooded them. They were got out safely . . . . Charing Cross and Waterloo Stations [are] closed. Time bombs are a nuisance. Streets have temporarily to be roped off . . . I cannot sleep while the raids are booming and crashing . . . . Tremendous lot of glass broken, e.g. Regent Street by time bomb. **(Thomas Jones,** *A Diary with Letters***)**

Do you know, or can you work out, what a "time bomb" is?

A LOCAL PAPER REPORTS THE BLITZ

Thursday, November 7th, 1940
Beckenham and Penge Advertiser
INTENSE BOMBING
Damage to Residential Property

For the first time for some weeks the outskirts of London enjoyed a week-end almost free from the disturbing effects of air-raids, and attacks of enemy planes were few . . . . In some parts of the suburbs an entirely peaceful Sunday and night were enjoyed . . .

. . . [In the early hours of the previous Friday] Mr. and Mrs. H. Cocksedge . . . were sleeping under the stairs as a refuge.

Towns on which more than 50 tons of high-explosive were dropped in raids, December 1940 and January 1941

December, 1940	January, 1941
London	London
Liverpool-Birkenhead	Avonmouth
Manchester	Bristol
Sheffield	Portsmouth
Birmingham	Cardiff
Bristol	Manchester
Southampton	Swansea
Portsmouth	Derby
	Southampton

Towns at the top of the list were most severely raided; towns at the bottom least severely. Can you work out any reasons for bombing these particular towns?

> Mr. Cocksedge is a cripple ... and when Mrs. Cocksedge heard the bomb falling she threw herself over her husband as he was sleeping, and protected him from the falling debris. They were both badly shaken but uninjured. They have now lost their home as a result of this misfortune. Their pets, a cat and dog, disappeared and were probably killed. Mrs. Cocksedge speaks with much gratitude of the kindness of neighbours in assisting them and other victims of the bombing.

On the same page of the *Advertiser* as the bombing report, an enterprising local tradesman was offering:

> Emergency Repairs
> Given Speedy Attention by
> MANSELL LTD.
> Roofs temporarily covered the same day if advised by 10.0 a.m. Full repairs can follow with a minimum of delay. Offices open for emergency calls on Sundays from 9.0 a.m.-12.0 (noon)

THE BLITZ OUTSIDE LONDON

As you can see from the table, other large towns also became targets for the German bombers (Hull, for example, had 86 major raids in all, and 85% of its housing was damaged). In Birmingham, one woman kept a record of her experiences for the survey organization called "Mass Observation":

> Nov. 19 [1940]
> 5.30 p.m. .... I had cooked a dinner and was about to serve it up when the sirens went.
> Les [husband] came in and found Jacq and I sitting in the cubby hole. I said 'I'll just dish the dinner up when the planes have slacked off for a moment'. They didn't slack off, they got worse, a terrific bombardment started and then the house shook with bombs exploding. Les said 'Dinner or no dinner we're going down to the shelter, I hope you've bailed it out'. We scrambled into our clothes, carried a blanket and cushions and hoped for the best. The sky was one blaze of light, gunfire was going on and did we run.
> We all got in safely, the floor was one large puddle, we sorted ourselves out and made the best of it ... (Quoted in Tom Harrison's *Living Through the Blitz*)
>
> The daughter, Jacq, was 11. They had the dinner at 2.30 a.m.

What do you think would have been the worst things about life during the Blitz? How did people try to protect themselves? (You can find out a good deal about this from the extracts in this section and the next.)

Escape from the Bombs

The Blitz drove many homeless or frightened families to take refuge with relatives in safe areas. Others just found themselves the best shelters available. Some families slept for months on London Underground station platforms. People who were not affected by the bombing did their best to help those who were.

CHISLEHURST CAVES PROVIDE SHELTER

When thousands of South London people arrived to shelter in the caves at Chislehurst in Kent, the Rector of St Nicholas Church appealed for help:

> The migration to the Caves has brought to our doors a splendid chance of service, for nearly 5,000 South Londoners are there .... Helpers are wanted in the kitchen at the Rest House from 10 to 2 each day, where we serve anything from 80 to 200 hot dinners .... Helpers are wanted for the canteen, where about 1,000 cups of tea are made each night. Call at the canteen in the Caves ... round about 6 o'clock, taking with you two or three rugs (for a night in a deck-chair) and being prepared to share the morning duty at 5 a.m. ... Gifts of old clothing for men and women are wanted ... (Rector's Letter, St Nicholas Parish Magazine, October 1940)

Can you think of any reasons why the gifts of clothing might be needed?

Here Helmuth Weissenborn shows part of the East End of London after a bad air-raid. Notice the firemen with their water pump and hose. Where are all the local people? (A sign on the left suggests one possible place.)

A SHROPSHIRE FAMILY TAKES IN RELATIVES

Margaret Gibbons, who wrote down her memories for this book, lived with her parents and younger brother in a small, four-roomed house in Shrewsbury. She was ten years old when the household suddenly increased in size:

> One evening in November 1940, about 6 p.m. my aunt and 18 month old daughter almost fell into the house. Their faces and clothes were black as they had walked to the station in Birmingham through streets lined with blazing buildings. It was the third day of bombing, my aunt's husband had just been called up and she got away in desperation. About two months after that another aunt arrived with her three daughters aged 6, 3 and 12 months ... from an inner city area of Liverpool. They had been sheltering in the cellar of their home, the children in cots suspended from the ceiling. The

eldest had been flung out of hers, and suffered from acute stuttering.... They came to us when my uncle was called up. For about 4 months there were 10 of us in our small house. We managed, because the children were very young. My parents and brother shared one bedroom and we put up two beds in the other — one shared between my younger aunt and me, the other by the aunt and her three daughters. The 18 month-old baby was accommodated cosily in a large drawer which was removed from the chest and put on top of it....

The whole district was filled already with children brought in mainly from the Liverpool area, so we were only a little more overcrowded than other neighbours.

The aunt from Birmingham went home after 6 months but the remaining eight of us stayed together until the end of the war....

You have probably spotted the reason why Margaret Gibbons' two aunts especially needed help and support from their relations at this time (what had happened to both their husbands?)

A NARROW ESCAPE FOR MUSLIMS IN CARDIFF

People could not spend all their time in shelters, yet even going to a religious service could be dangerous. The *Cardiff Times* reported on 8 February 1941, that about 30 Muslims

> were praying at the Mosque at the rear of the Islamic Headquarters when the buildings were hit. Barefooted they made their way out over the wreckage and rubble to safety.

Cardiff had a racially-mixed population and was visited by ships from all over the world. When King George VI visited the city in 1941 he was introduced to a group of A.R.P. workers containing representatives of 14 nationalities.

This is what it was like to have your street bombed.

School Life

Schooling was disrupted for many children. Evacuated schools often had to share buildings with local country schools. In the large towns, some school buildings were damaged by bombing, and lessons were constantly interrupted by trips to the shelters. Teachers and children made the best of things, however, and also tried to help the war effort.

DIFFICULTIES FOR LONDON SCHOOLS DURING THE BLITZ

Eighteen East London elementary schools were reopened on Monday, December 15th [1940]. The recent house-to-house canvassing undertaken to encourage evacuation revealed that there were 2,680 children of school age still in Stepney and Whitechapel, and 2,800 in Poplar and Bow.... The decision to open the schools having been taken, it was necessary to find schools still in a habitable state.... But several schools have been completely destroyed, and others badly damaged,

◀ *Rules about uniform have been relaxed for these London grammar-school girls. Their school still insists on a hat or beret being worn — but look at the variety of coats and scarves.*

WAR BRINGS CHANGES

Reports in the *Times Educational Supplement* show how schools had to adapt to war-time conditions:

TYNEMOUTH   12 October 1940
The Education Committee has decided that in the event of an air raid after 7 p.m. schools will start the following day at 9.45 a.m. instead of 9 a.m.

DURHAM   1 March 1941
The City Education Committee's first school canteen has been opened at Blue Coat School by Alderman W. Smith.... Alderman Smith expressed the view that canteens would become one of the chief activities of school life, because a child could not benefit from education unless he was properly fed.

while a number are still occupied by civil defence units. Hardly a school had escaped unscathed, and those that could be re-opened after minor repairs had to have suitable shelters.... A small percentage of children have been completely without schooling for 12 months, but the majority only since the beginning of September; all have settled down well and seem glad to be back.... (Report from *Times Educational Supplement's* Special Correspondent, 21 December 1940)

When and why had schools been closed? (Look back to pages 14-15 if you cannot think of the answer.) Why do you think the children were "glad to be back"? Notice that the schools are called "elementary schools" — you might like to find out what kind of schools these were.

SCHOOL UNIFORMS 29 November 1941
The Board of Education... point out that parents are finding difficulty in meeting their children's needs out of the coupon limits allowed and authorities and governing bodies are asked to take immediate steps to see that regulations requiring distinctive clothing [*uniforms*] to be worn are rescinded, and that reasonable discretion is allowed to parents in the matter of providing clothes for children at schools of all types....

Which of these changes had the biggest long-term effect on the schools? (Ask yourself which has been carried on in schools right up to the present day.)

A COUNTRY SCHOOL IN WAR-TIME

Schools record daily activities in their log-books. Here are some entries from the log-book of Boughton Monchelsea School, Kent. (Is your school old enough to have a war-time log-book?)

1939
Dec. 23 During the week, a carol party of native children and evacuated children collected £6.11.5 for a wool fund — girls to make knitted comforts for men serving in the forces.

1940
Aug. 16 During air-raids this week the fall of bombs and the rattle of machine guns could be heard distinctly. Many enemy aircraft have passed over the school.

1942
Mar. 20 School display of warships made by the children

1943
Jun. 17 Miss Smith visited the School this morning to judge 'Wings for Victory' posters and models.

1944
Jun. 16 Attendance poor owing to attack of pilotless planes
(Extracts from Denis Tye, *Boughton Monchelsea School*, and Denis Tye, *A Village School 1850-1970 Boughton Monchelsea*)

Notice how the war provides some topics for the children's work. "Wings for Victory" weeks were held to collect money for National Savings, which the posters suggested the government could use to buy aeroplanes. You can find out about the "pilotless planes" on pages 40-41.

University Life

The Universities managed to keep going during the war, though many of their staff went off to fight or into government work (some helped to crack codes or do other kinds of intelligence work). There were fewer men students than before the war, and most of these could only stay for a year or two before being called up. As conscription for women did not begin until late in 1941, there were more girls free to study; but many students did part-time war work of some kind or another during their University terms.

DOUBTS ABOUT THE FUTURE, 1940

WAR-TIME OXFORD
PROSPECTS FOR NEXT TERM
A brief statement of the facts may help to resolve, in the minds of parents and schoolmasters, the doubts raised by rumour as to what kind of University, if any, there will be next term. One has even heard the question, "Is there going to be a next term?" . . . (*Times Educational Supplement,* **14 September 1940**)

Oxford advised prospective students to come, pointing out that men were likely to have at least one year there, possibly more, and that shortened courses (2-year Honours Degree courses instead of 3-year) were available.

A LONDON COLLEGE IS EVACUATED

Margaret Crane joined King's College, London University, in October 1940, to study English. The College English Department had been evacuated to Bristol. She remembers:

Bristol was bombed while we were there: we used to go down to the cellars of our Hall of Residence. We wore trousers over our pyjamas during night raids (but never in day-time or in the street — trousers were not thought respectable for girl students at that time)

One night in my first term King's College Arts library, which was occupying the Great Hall of Bristol University, was set on fire by incendiaries and completely destroyed. Soon after that we were sent home, for an extended Christmas vacation. There was nowhere for us to work without the library space.

Later, students were on a rota for firewatching. We usually did one night a week, on duty for two hours at a stretch, two of us together, working as part of a team. Those off duty slept in camp beds . . . . The most exciting place to watch was the room at the top of the tower of the University building. You could see the whole of Bristol.

You can check some of Margaret Crane's memories against the report made by the University of Bristol in the *Times Educational Supplement*, 15 February 1941:

THE UNIVERSITIES IN WAR-TIME
Bristol
The fall in the undergraduate population from over 1,000 two years ago to under 800 at present — a figure which dwindles as men are called up — would not be apparent to an uninstructed observer, for the University buildings have never before been so full, owing chiefly to the migration into them of . . . King's College, London . . . . It cannot be said that the conditions of work have been comfortable or easy for either visitors or hosts, and since the buildings were damaged by enemy air raids which destroyed the Great Hall with the part of King's College Library housed in it, the strain upon accommodation has been very severe . . .

What can you learn about student life in Bristol from these two accounts? Which incident is described in both?

LOOKING AHEAD

Young men, in particular, knew that when they left University it would be to go to war. Sidney Keyes studied History at Oxford 1940-42. He also wrote poems. In March 1942, he expressed his feelings about the war and his own future:

WAR POET
I am the man who looked for peace and found
My own eyes barbed.
I am the man who groped for words and found
An arrow in my hand.
I am the builder whose firm walls surround
A slipping land.
When I grow sick or mad
Mock me not nor chain me:
When I reach for the wind
Cast me not down:
Though my face is a burnt book
And a wasted town.

Sidney Keyes joined the army in April 1942. In March 1943 he was sent to North Africa. A fortnight later, he was taken prisoner. He died "from unknown causes" in April 1943, aged not quite 21.

Service Life

Men and women who joined the armed forces had to adjust to a very different way of life from the one they were used to. They had to live in crowded conditions with complete strangers. As soon as they got used to being in one place, they might be moved on to another. They never knew when the time would come for them to be sent abroad to the battlefields. Meanwhile they often had boring work or training to do in Britain.

In August 1939 a letter to The Times *expressed the hope that "the girls now going into the Forces will not be encouraged to wear masculine trappings like trousers . . .". Service-women found trousers comfortable and practical: Molly Cooke wears them in this photograph.*

EARLY DAYS IN THE A.T.S.

Molly Cooke volunteered for the A.T.S. in November 1939. As you can see from her description (written for this book) of her first months of service, accommodation for so many new recruits was not easy to find.

I worked in one of the offices at the R.A.O.C. depot at Didcot, known as P.4. We were in civilian billets and had our meals in camp. The civilians did not take kindly to women in uniform in the early days, maybe this was partly the reason for moving us into what had been the Coronet Cinema. There were 3 or 4 rows of beds down the main part of the hall, and the N.C.O. on duty slept on the stage. My next move was to the Vicarage with a few others . . . .

I got very frustrated just sorting tickets all day, I felt I should be doing something more useful and I eventually managed to get moved to the telephone exchange at the depot . . . . I really enjoyed this work which I continued to do for the duration. Because we did shift work we all had to live in barracks. They can still be seen as you pass through Didcot in the train . . . . From Didcot I went to Bicester in charge of the new switchboard that had been put in the R.A.O.C. depot there. We lived in Nissen huts at a camp within walking distance of the depot . . .

Notice how Molly Cooke uses army abbreviations like "N.C.O." (you'll find these in the glossary, page 45, if you don't know them already) and war-time expressions like "for the duration".

LIFE IN AN ARMY CAMP

The poet Alun Lewis spent two years in army camps in England. He wrote stories and poems describing camp life.

> Eight in a tent, lying on ground sheets, feet to the tentpole, kit piled high and in small space by one's side. Writing letters, looking at snaps, cutting toe-nails, sewing buttons, contemplating something distant, brooding over something immediate.... The other seven don't notice, don't interfere.
>
> In the Army you begin again. All you were seems to have vanished. It was simply another mode of life. Civvy street. I was a schoolmaster in a big secondary school, a responsible .. job. Now I clean latrines, windows, barrack rooms...
> (From "Lance-Jack", a short story)

> All day it has rained, and we on the edge of the moors
> Have sprawled in our bell-tents, moody and dull as boors,
> Groundsheets and blankets spread on the muddy ground
> And from the first grey wakening we have found
> No refuge from the skirmishing fine rain
> And the wind that made the canvas heave and flap
> And the taut wet guy-ropes ravel out and snap...
> (From "All Day It Has Rained")

War-artist Carel Weight painted a series of pictures called Recruit's Progress. Here he sees the funny side of life in a crowded barrack-room.
▼

Both Alun Lewis and Molly Cooke were later sent overseas. Lewis was killed in an accident in Burma, but Molly Cooke returned safely after serving in Holland and Germany.

You might like to use the material on these pages to make up a story (or a letter home) about life in the army for a new recruit.

War Work

Work in the factories and mines was as important as service with the armed forces. Ernest Bevin, Minister of Labour, won Trade Union support. Long hours were worked — sometimes 60 hours a week for men and 55 for women. From 1941 men over 41 (that is, over conscription age) and young, unmarried women had to register at a Labour Exchange. They could then be directed to take a job vital to the war-effort. Later this also applied to women between 19 and 50.

WOMEN REGISTER FOR WORK

A woman clerk in a Welsh Labour Exchange has described for this book the reactions to registration of women:

> Married women with children were not 'required' to take a job [*i.e. it was not compulsory*]. And women past their early forties were registered but never 'required' to take employment. It occurs to me that women over forty were considered 'past it'. Indeed the very idea of registering them aroused great opposition. But . . . it was from these two groups, the volunteers, that the vast majority of munition workers were recruited.
>
> They literally jumped at the idea of going into industry. They were emancipated! At a stroke. Freed from the grinding poverty of the '30s, released from the kitchen sink, they had a life — and money of their own . . . . The registration of the over 40s caused great interest in a small town like ours . . . . The staff experienced some surprises . . . . Indeed it was not unknown for us to be asked if a particular person had registered yet . . . .

(All secrets were kept, however.)

NEW WORKERS IN THE FACTORIES

The figures on the right, from the *Annual Report of the Chief Inspector of Factories, 1941,* show how many accidents there were in the factories in the early years of the war. Study the figures, then read the Chief Inspector's comments.

Women were now needed to do work previously done by men. By 1943, 40% of employees in the aircraft industry were female. Notice the way the "ideal" factory worker in this poster does her hair.

Reportable accidents

Year	Adult Males	Adult Females
1938	134,752	14,626
1939	146,417	17,029
1940	173,228	23,766
1941	191,343	42,857
Percentage increase of 1941 over 1938	42%	192%

... we see that the main increase is in accidents to adult women — a sign that during this year not only did women take up a great share in the work of making munitions, but that they also took up their share of the dangerous processes ...
... Perhaps the most distressing accident that occurs to females is that due to hair becoming entangled in moving machinery ... 179 accidents due to this cause occurred during 1941 ... special efforts ... have been made to secure improvements in the fencing [of machines]. When this has been done, caps can be a help .... Unfortunately the modern style of hairdressing does not lend itself to the hair being carefully covered and in spite of much advice from Inspectors and others the fluffy curl still protrudes ...

Why did women not take the advice to cover their heads? What main reason does the Inspector give for the increased number of accidents to women? There was an increase in accidents to men also — why, do you think?

LOOKING AFTER THE WORKERS

It was essential to keep workers in industry fit and healthy. The next extract records one of the improvements in working conditions that came about during the war:

... the attitude of employers and workers to the need for canteens has changed considerably ... workers who had earlier stated they did not require a hot meal and would not use a canteen, have demanded canteen facilities: the tightening of rationing, the increased employment of women, and especially of married women, the operation of shift systems, the adoption of shorter meal times to enable the worker to get home earlier, and the big scale transfer of workers to towns away from home, often into billets, have been factors determining this altered attitude. In some cases enemy action has had its effect too ... at a large shipyard ... most of the workers lived very near, and the demand [for a canteen] was not great; but heavy bombing damaged the workers' homes and they had to go and live in widely scattered districts and were no longer able to get home for meals. This led to demands at the works ... [where two canteens were soon established]
(*Annual Report of the Chief Inspector of Factories, 1941*)

Before the war, few work places had canteens. By late 1941, there were more than 6,000 at factories, docks and building-sites.

Draw up your own petition to a factory-owner or works-manager, asking for a war-time canteen.

Helping the War-Effort

People wanted to help win the war. Many did voluntary work in their spare time. Families responded to government demands to salvage anything that could be re-used. Left-over food, vegetable peelings, etc, went into "pig-bins" to be collected for use on farms as animal-feed.

SCHOOL-CHILDREN'S HOLIDAY ACTIVITIES

HOLIDAY WAR WORK
DEVON CHILDREN'S CAMPAIGN
[The children] are covering a wide range of useful tasks — protecting windows against blast, removing ration coupons for the local grocer, tidying the village street, darning socks for soldiers, looking after babies, carrying meals to the harvest field, making signalling flags for soldiers, and digging tank-traps, cleaning Home Guard rifles, preparing ricks, thatching a hayrick, sheep-dipping, hoeing turnips, driving cattle, milking and dairy work, harvesting .... Collecting has been another main activity .... The children have ... retrieved over 4,000 lb of bones and an incredible amount of metal, rags, jars, bottles, tinfoil, paper, and cardboard; the aluminium alone filled five sacks ..
(*Times Literary Supplement*, 14 September 1940)

Notice the date: why were the children digging tank-traps? (Look back at pages 12-13 if you don't remember).

A.P.L. 5

"PHOTOGRAPHS,"
ADMIRALTY,
LONDON, S.W.1

Ref No 50826
Date 3-9-43

We return herewith the material you were good enough to loan us for copying. Your contribution to our files is greatly appreciated.

Ordinary people helped the war-effort in unexpected ways. This document refers to holiday snapshots sent in response to a government appeal (they were of the North African coast — the Date List will tell you why they were needed). A man who worked in Military Intelligence wrote that "for much of our knowledge ... we had to depend on picture postcards and family snapshots .... How strange it seemed sometimes, as one studied some old-fashioned photograph showing a French family taking its luncheon on the beach ... that the reason why this particular photograph was of particular interest was that it showed with extreme clarity the gradient of the beach at the exact point where our tanks would disembark ..." (Goronwy Rees, *A Bundle of Sensations*)

Saving helped the war-effort. The government could use the money, and the less people spent, the lower prices were in the shops. In this advertisement the wicked "squander-bug" is shown tempting someone to spend.

FIVE TIMES MORE THAN IT'S WORTH – IT'S A LOVELY WASTE OF MONEY

...HAT YOU BUY IS HITLER'S BUSINESS

..., more than ever before, every available penny is needed ...he war effort. By wasting money you are helping the ...is to 'hold up' the day of victory. Join the forces of ...k instead, by putting all you can each week into War ...ngs.

...GS CERTIFICATES • DEFENCE BONDS • POST OFFICE AND TRUSTEE SAVINGS BANKS

Issued by the National Savings Committee

The W.V.S.

By early September 1939, 370,000 women had already joined the Women's Voluntary Services; another 96,000 joined during the first month of the war. This report of their activities was given by the head of the Beckenham (Kent) branch in April 1941:

"WASTE NOT, WANT NOT"

The Ministry of Information often gave advice on avoiding waste. The following notice appeared in newspapers in March 1941:

> What do I do . . .
>   to make sure that my
>   kitchen scraps are not wasted?
>
> I put them aside for pig food, but I take care that no bits of glass, china or metal are mixed with them . . . I know that bones yield glycerine for explosives, glue and fertilizers, so I keep these separate also. If I can boil them till they are as clean as a whistle (and get nourishing soup from them first) so much the better. Even if I let my dog gnaw them, they will still be useful as war material.

What do you think you could have done to help the war-effort if you had lived then?

> . . . In their work for the troops there was much that they could do . . . in providing canteens for the service clubs, and also in washing and mending for the men . . . . The members of the W.V.S. helped with the canteens at the A.R.P. depots, and gave assistance in the making of the nets used for camouflaging, and many volunteered for humble duties which in their own homes were done for them . . . .
> There was also the work of distributing clothing to those bombed out of their homes . . . .

Can you tell from anything in this description what kind of people W.V.S. members in this area were?

Censorship and Propaganda

In war-time, news is usually withheld if it might help the enemy, and this was certainly done in Britain in the Second World War. Sometimes, unpleasant truths were not revealed for a long time, in case they caused panic among the British people. On the other hand, the press, the radio and posters were all used to encourage people to do what the government wanted — and to discourage undesirable or dangerous activities. Slogans like "Careless Talk Costs Lives" were repeated on poster after poster to drive the message home — in this case, that you might give information to an enemy spy without meaning to.

HOLDING BACK NEWS

Long suppressed information on the activities of the fly-bomb issued last week was read with keen interest by residents of this much bombed area. (*Beckenham & Penge Advertiser*, **14 September 1944**)

What reasons can you think of for not revealing details (such as place-names) of flying-bomb incidents? Why do you think it was the custom to speak and write of an "incident" when a bomb fell — instead of using a word like "disaster" or "explosion"? (You will find out more about this kind of bomb on pages 40-41.)

ENCOURAGING GOOD BEHAVIOUR

Here is one of the verses produced for London Transport's "Billy Brown of London Town" posters. See if you can pick out the things that the poster is trying to get people to do — and to prevent them from doing.

WORKING FOR THE PROPAGANDA MACHINE

Many writers produced material for propaganda films, radio programmes or articles — using stories that would cheer people up, or make them want to be brave, or showing the enemy in the worst possible light. George Orwell was one of these writers and this is what he said about the job:

To compose a propaganda pamphlet or a radio feature needs just as much work as to write something you believe in, with the difference that the finished product is worthless.

Why did Orwell consider his propaganda work "worthless"?

Billy Brown's own Highway Code
For blackouts is 'Stay off the Road',
He'll never step out and begin
To meet a bus that's pulling in.
He doesn't wave his torch at night,
But 'flags' his bus with something white.
He never jostles in a queue,
But waits and takes his turn. DO YOU?
(December 1940)

What is the advantage of putting messages to the public into verse?

You will find a number of persuasive government posters and printed messages in other sections of this book: study them, and decide which you think are the most effective.

The little things . . .

Malta,
Little Island
that would not yield
to savage might.
Immortal symbol
of all little things
which, having faith
and courage
and endurance
shall prevail
against the dark
destroying powers.
Little squadrons—
how little
once—
that charged
into big formations
and scattered them.
Little ships
that fought through
tempest of flame
and sea
to bring supplies.
Little homes
shattered ;
Humble folk
carrying on
in Malta . . .
as in Britain . . .
Island to Island . . .
calling . . .
'Carry on.'

◀ *This National Savings advertisement of 1943 holds up the example of Malta, an island under British rule which bravely resisted German attacks. In what ways might the message appeal to ordinary savers? Notice how words like "little" and "humble" are used to describe people on the British side. What words are used to describe the enemy?*

You can have an interesting discussion on the subject of propaganda and censorship. Is it right to use them in war-time? and if so, what rules would you make about their use? Is it right ever to use them in peacetime? How much, in fact, are people influenced by propaganda?

This war is being fought for the rights of little things — the sacred right of little folk to live their lives unmolested by big gangsters. It is being won by millions of little sacrifices, little efforts — and millions doing their 'bit.' Our duty is to make our 'bit' bigger — which means, here and now, work harder and SAVE MORE.

. . . Wings for Victory

Issued by the National Savings Committee

Food

Food rationing began in January 1940, when sugar, butter and bacon were rationed. Meat followed in March, and tea, fats and margarine in July. As non-rationed foods became scarce, people found it more and more difficult to stretch their food supply to feed their family. Not surprisingly, everyone thought a lot about food.

GETTING EXTRA FOOD

However clever or rich you were, you had to try to make your rations last you a week. You were lucky if, like the writer Virginia Woolf, you had a friend who owned a farm. Then you might get a very welcome present:

> ... All I can say is that when we discovered the butter in the envelope box, we had in ... Louie [the maid] ... to look. That's a whole pound of butter I said. Saying which, I broke off a lump and ate it pure. Then in the glory of my heart I gave all our week's ration — which is about the size of my thumb nail — to Louie ... then sat down and ate bread and butter .... Think of our lunch tomorrow! ... in the middle of the table I shall put the whole pat. And I shall say: Eat as much as you like ... (Virginia Woolf to Vita Sackville West, November 1940, quoted in *Virginia Woolf*, vol. 2, by Quentin Bell)

By November 1940 the butter ration had gone down to 2oz per person per week. Cut a modern 250 gm package of butter into four, and you'll have some idea how much this was. Then see if you can make one piece last a week.

WAR-TIME RECIPES

Housewives were given plenty of advice on war-time cookery by the B.B.C., by the Ministry of Food and by almost every newspaper and magazine. This 1944 recipe, from the Parish Magazine of St Nicholas, Chislehurst, Kent, is typical:

> NO FAT — For a war-time currant loaf, take ½ lb. self-raising flour, half a cupful of dried fruit (any kind), 2ozs of sugar, 1oz. of egg powder, milk. Mix ... put in cake tin, bake for one hour in a fairly hot oven.

The "egg powder" was usually called "dried egg": real eggs were in such short supply that most people could get only about one a fortnight.

The next recipe in this issue of the magazine was for *Potato and Jam Pudding* — to serve with custard. How would that taste, do you think? You can understand why the author William Plomer wrote the following verse about food in war-time, and the helpful hints provided by the Ministry of Food.

Girls in the A.T.S. (see page 22) took just as much interest in their supply of food as Virginia Woolf did, in her comfortable house in Sussex. Molly Cooke remembers:

> at the time of Dunkirk ... my mother had sent me a food parcel so we gorged jam tarts in the garden ... we liked to go [to Oxford] for a decent meal, we seemed to live on baked beans in camp, I suppose that is why I don't like them now. There was also a good cafe in Didcot where we used to go for tea, they had lush Kunzel cakes ...

Ah, that ingenious Ministry of Food!
It may be clever, but it is not good
To turn potatoes into jam, and dine
On offal, oats and home made cabbage wine.
What do I do when I am told to try
A groundsel salad, or a toadstool pie?
I fast for victory. It is not nice
To take the Ministry of Food's advice.

W.P. 1942

Look in old cookery books for war-time recipes: most families made "mock cream" (one recipe for this used blancmange mixed with margarine) and had to learn to cook with dried egg and little or no fat.

This advice from the Ministry of Food was printed in a women's magazine in 1943. Which (unrationed) vegetable is used to fill out both packed lunches?

One from each of these Three

1 For Body-building

Some fillings and stuffings.

MEAT, CHEESE, FISH, CANNED PILCHARDS, CANNED PINK SALMON. Season, sometimes add a dash of sauce, and mash.

DRIED BEANS OR PEAS. Soak 12-24 hours and cook, then mash and mix with grated cheese or household milk, flavour with meat or with vegetable or meat extract. Canned beans in brine are already cooked and cost no points.

DRIED EGG. Mix in usual way, put in a greased basin, cook in a saucepan of boiling water for 15 minutes. Turn out and chop.

2 For Energy

BUTTER, MARGARINE, DRIPPING.

BAKED POTATOES. Scrub and prick with a fork before cooking.

BOILED POTATOES. Choose firm ones, cook in skins, peel, split (or if very large slice thickly) and use as covers for " sandwiches."

POTATO PASTRY. Use for turnovers or cut into squares for sandwiches — jam, fruit or savoury.

HOME-MADE POTATO SCONES.

BREAD, FLOUR. But please be sparing with both, to save shipping space.

3 For Protection

A SALAD. Shredded raw vegetables with a little seasoning and dressing or vinegar.

A BUNCH OF WATERCRESS.

A FEW NEW TURNIPS, PEELED; SOME YOUNG CARROTS. MUSTARD AND CRESS.

COARSELY CHOPPED PARSLEY, CHOPPED GREEN TOPS OF SPRING ONIONS to sprinkle in sandwiches.

FRUIT when in season.

Suggestions for 2 Packed Lunches

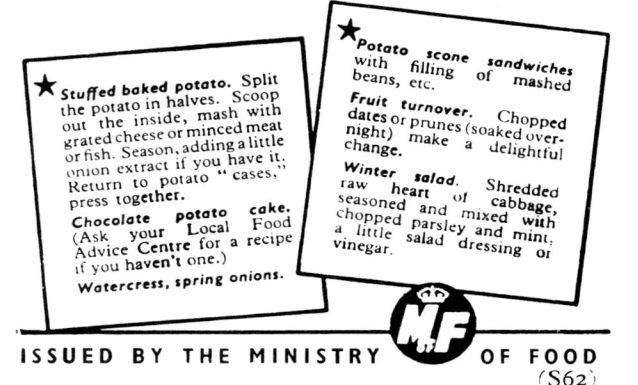

★ **Stuffed baked potato.** Split the potato in halves. Scoop out the inside, mash with grated cheese or minced meat or fish. Season, adding a little onion extract if you have it. Return to potato " cases," press together.

Chocolate potato cake. (Ask your Local Food Advice Centre for a recipe if you haven't one.)

Watercress, spring onions.

★ **Potato scone sandwiches** with filling of mashed beans, etc.

Fruit turnover. Chopped dates or prunes (soaked overnight) make a delightful change.

Winter salad. Shredded raw heart of cabbage, seasoned and mixed with chopped parsley and mint, a little salad dressing or vinegar.

ISSUED BY THE MINISTRY OF FOOD
(S62)

What on earth can I pack for his lunch tomorrow ?

Well, there are still plenty of things with which you can make up a packed lunch that is tasty and satisfying, and nourishing, too. The point to remember is that a packed lunch, like any other meal, should be " balanced." That is, it should contain some body-building food, some energy-giving food, and some health-protecting food, with, of course, the all-important vitamins.

No food falls *completely* into any single one of these groups, but choose one item from each of the three paragraphs below, and you can be sure of having packed a good balanced meal, and a tasty one, too.

Clothes

Clothes rationing began on 1 June 1941. At first, the allowance was 66 coupons per person for a year (later it was reduced). People wore their old clothes for as long as possible. They made new things out of them too: mothers cut their old dresses up into blouses for their daughters. "Make Do and Mend" became a war-time slogan. Simple clothes which did not use much material were produced, especially after the government introduced "Utility" clothing. "Utility" clothes were price-controlled and therefore cheaper to buy (though at the time young people did not think them very glamorous).

RATIONING PROBLEMS TO BE SOLVED

Special arrangements had to be made for people with special needs. For example, mothers were given an allowance of 50 coupons for a new baby (just as well, because one coupon had to be given up for each nappy). There were problems for workers too:

> House of Commons, 11th June 1941
> Mr. Rhys Davies:
> Will the Parliamentary Secretary bear in mind that one pair of boots a year for a coal miner, steel smelter or quarry man is impossible?
> (Answer: Yes, Sir)
>
> House of Commons, 9th September 1941
> President of the Board of Trade:
> It has now been decided to issue 60 coupons a year to all underground workers in the [coal] industry to meet their special needs in excess of those covered by the ordinary civilian ration of 66 coupons . . .
> (Extracts from *Hansard*, 1941)

Why would workers in heavy industries need more clothes?

ISSUED BY THE BOARD OF TRADE

EXTRA WEAR from childrens wear

NOWADAYS every re-made garment becomes a uniform of honour and every darn a "decoration." The only thing that really matters is to keep a child *cosily* clad. Here are some practical hints that you may be able to turn to good account.

MOTHERS CAN LEARN FROM OTHERS

It is surprising how much extra wear can be got out of children's clothes by "reinforcement" at the right places. For example:

'Anchorage' for buttons A sudden tug often brings away a button and a bit of material too. This is less likely to happen if you "back" each button with a small circle of material on the wrong side of the garment, and sew well through.

Double strength for sleeves Schoolgirls' blouses and pyjama jackets usually "go" first under the arms. Put an extra "half" lining here from scrap material when making them, to provide a basis for easy mending.

New clothes from old From a man's discarded shirt, enough sound material can be salvaged to make a school blouse for a small girl. Father's old flannel trousers provide stuff for a warm little frock; use the top part for the bodice and make a gored skirt from the leg portions. Trim with contrasting collar and cuffs.

Urgent—BEWARE THE MOTH Now is the time to start your campaign against the moth grub. It's no good waiting until you see moths flying about; *it's the grub that eats your clothes*. Beat, brush and shake your clothes, especially those you haven't been wearing lately, and if possible air them out of doors.

Mend and Make-do to save buying new

SHOPS PREPARE FOR CLOTHES RATIONING

Clothing coupons could be spent in any shop, so there was keen competition to get customers. One Croydon store, Grants, put a series of advertisements in local papers in June stressing

With the Rationing of Clothes it will be QUALITY THAT COUNTS

Gorringes, a London store, advertised the goods in its Sale starting Monday 30 June 1941 with coupon values given as well as prices:

WOOL BLOUSES AT HALF PRICE
Sale Price 15/-
5 coupons each

◀ Some government advice published in newspapers on how to make children's clothes last longer.

SPENDING YOUR CLOTHES COUPONS

Try to decide how you would have spent the 66 coupons in the first year of clothes rationing (remember you would have some clothes already — but these might be wearing out). Here is a list of coupon values to help you:

Women

coat or raincoat	14 coupons
dress	11 "
pyjamas	8 "
nightdress	6 "
vest	3 "
skirt	7 "
trousers	8 "
briefs	2 "
stockings	2 per pair
shoes	5 " "

Men

overcoat or raincoat	16 coupons
blazer	13 "
trousers	8 "
shirt	8 "
underpants	4 "
shoes	7 "

Children's clothes cost fewer coupons, because they would soon grow out of them and have to have more.

MAKING DO

Shops selling luxury goods had little to offer customers, so they provided repair services instead. See how cleverly Jayes of Croydon, a shop which sold fur coats, tried to tempt its customers at least to bring old coats in to be repaired or altered:

Like other clothing firms, Braemar (makers of woollen sweaters, etc) wanted to keep its customers. What service was it offering them during clothes-rationing?

Notice the uniform worn by the girls in the picture. They belong to the Women's Land Army, who worked on farms instead of joining the forces.

'*Your* Braemars always look so new'
'*A stitch-in-time's**
what makes them do'

* Braemar can help you to 'mend and make-do', for their 'Stitch-in-time' Service has already repaired thousands of Braemars. If you have any Braemar garments that need mending, patching or re-shaping, just take them along to your nearest Braemar shop and the 'Stitch-in-time' Service will do the rest.

All garments must be sent through a retailer, please!

BRAEMAR

Innes, Henderson & Co. Ltd., Hawick, Scotland

JAYES
   The Furriers
      Save your Coupons
      And your Money for
      Victory
      Every Coupon saved means so much

Your old Fur Coat
Offers a solution to your problem.
UNRATIONED FUR REPAIRS,
Remodelling and Cleaning.

Coats reworked to look like new.
Old coats renovated
Unlimited styles to choose from.
Prices are keen and estimates free.
Obligations — there are none.
Now is the time — Don't hesitate —
Save your Coupons and look well
   dressed!
(*Beckenham and Penge Advertiser*,
12 June, 1941)

What kind of a person would you have to be, though, to have your clothing problem solved in this way? (It is worth remembering that some people were too poor even to use up all their 66 coupons: spare coupons were illegally sold on the "Black Market". The usual price was about 1/- per coupon.)

Separated Families

LETTER-WRITING

In November 1939, the Vicar of St Mary's, Plaistow, Kent reminded his parishioners of a very important war-time fact:

> ... don't forget to write regularly, especially to the lads on service, and write whether you get replies or not. Unless one has experienced it, one cannot understand the hunger for Home Letters. Also give plenty of news. Things that seem trivial to those at home assume a greater importance to one miles away ...

Millions of letters must have been written to and by men and women in the forces between 1939 and 1945. Perhaps, if you are lucky, someone in your family has kept letters from that period.

Most families had relatives in the armed services or at sea with the Merchant Navy. They kept in touch by letter and looked forward to periods of leave; but they faced constant anxiety. For those posted abroad, "embarkation leave" — the last contact with their families for most of them until the war ended — was a very emotional time.

A PRISONER OF WAR'S WIFE

Mrs Elizabeth Hayes, of Risca, Gwent, had a husband in the Merchant Navy. She wrote down her memories for this book:

> I heard the news from the British Tanker Company that Ewart's ship was sunk in January 1941. Six months later I heard from the B.T.C. that Ewart was picked up 500 miles S. West of Sierra Leone. The first card from him had a Bordeaux stamp. He was then taken to Munich and then to the naval camp Stalag 8.

Why were songs like these so popular in war-time?

Date	Name	Type	Gross tons	Position	Cause of loss
JANUARY, 1941					
2	NALGORA	S.	6,579	22°24'N. 21°11'W.	S.M.
3	PINEWOOD	S.	2,466	1½m. S. of Pier, Southend	Mine
5	SHAKESPEAR	S.	5,029	18°05'N, 21°10'W.	S.M.
6	LION*	Tug	87	320° 2½ cables from No. 5 Medway Buoy	Mine
7	H. H. PETTERSEN	S.	975	52°22'N. 02°05'E.	Mine
6	EMPIRE THUNDER	S.	5,965	59°14'N. 12°43'W.	S.M.
8	STRATHERN (Trinity House Tender)	M.	683	51°45'N. 01°10'E.	Mine
8	CLYTONEUS	M.	6,278	56°23'N. 15°24'W.	A.C.
9	BASSANO	S.	4,843	57°57'N. 17°42'W.	S.M.
10	MIDDLESEX	S.	9,583	198° 0.9m. from Flatholm Is.	Mine
11	BEACHY*	S.	1,600	53°29'N. 16°24'W.	A.C.
14	EUMAEUS	S.	7,472	08°55'N. 15°03'W.	S.M.
15	MANCUNIUM	Sludge Vessel	1,286	2m. N.E. of Bar L.V., Mersey	Mine
16	OROPESA	S.	14,118	56°28'N. 12°00'W.	S.M.
16	ZEALANDIC	S.	10,578	58°28'N. 20°43'W.	S.M.
17	ALMEDA STAR	S.	14,935	58°16'N. 13°40'W.	S.M.
18	BRITISH UNION*	M. Tank	6,987	26°34'N. 30°58'W.	Raider

He was allowed to send one letter and two postcards a month. I could write once a month and send a parcel via the Red Cross once every three months — in it any woollen clothes, like scarf, socks, helmet, and cigarettes and chocolate (my sweet ration) and handkerchiefs. I sent the most colourful handkerchiefs — the Drama group used them when putting on plays like 'Rose Marie' [a musical]. He was teaching the sailors [for City and Guild examinations] and I sent the books via the Bodleian Library, Oxford.

He was released by the Americans three days before V.E. Day and flown home in a Wellington bomber to a camp — where he was fitted with civilian clothes after being debugged (in his case no need of debugging!) I guessed that he would be on a train landing 2 a.m. on V.E. Day. Friends took me to Newport Station to meet him.

Notice how long it was before Mrs Hayes knew whether her husband was dead or alive.

Study the table of "British Merchant Vessels Lost or Damaged": you will be able to pick out Chief Engineer Hayes' ship (the type of ship and name of the shipping company are the clues). Count up the number of ships sunk in this short period.

◀ *A table from* British Merchant Vessels Lost or Damaged by Enemy Action during the Second World War *(an H.M.S.O. publication). You can see from this list exactly how these ships were sunk. Work out what the letters in the last-but-one column stand for. In the last column, T is for "torpedo", G for "gunfire" and B for "bomb".*

A family snapshot taken just before Glynn Jones ▶ *sent overseas. He did not see his baby daughter again for three years.*

A SOLDIER'S FAMILY

Margaret and Glynn Jones married in September 1939: Glynn had already been called up. For nearly two years, they saw each other only for short periods of leave. Then Glynn was sent to Northern Ireland and his wife decided to take their new baby daughter to join him. Today Margaret Jones remembers:

We arrived in Ireland and the next day the news came that the battalion was posted and he would soon have to move again. However we had a few weeks together before that happened.

In November 1941, Margaret brought the baby back from Ireland to join Glynn again, this time in Leominster, Hereford-Worcester.

We were there together about three or four months, in digs with a very kind landlady . . . . Then Glynn was moved again . . .

The photograph below was taken outside the "kind landlady's" house in Leominster.

In October 1942 Glynn had a few days embarkation leave. He was away for the rest of the war, fighting in North Africa and Italy.

35

Allies in Britain

Although Britain "stood alone" against Germany in 1940, she was helped by her colonies and the Dominions. More help came from people who had managed to escape when the Germans occupied their countries. After the United States came into the war at the end of 1941, American servicemen too came to Britain.

WEST INDIANS COME TO HELP BRITAIN

Jamaica alone sent about 7,000 men to serve with the British armed forces. Workers came too: lumbermen from British Honduras to work in forests in Scotland, and over 300 West Indians to make munitions and aircraft in Northern factories. Some stayed when the war ended and settled into their local communities.

In answer to a question in the House of Commons in 1941, Mr George Hall expressed the government's gratitude:

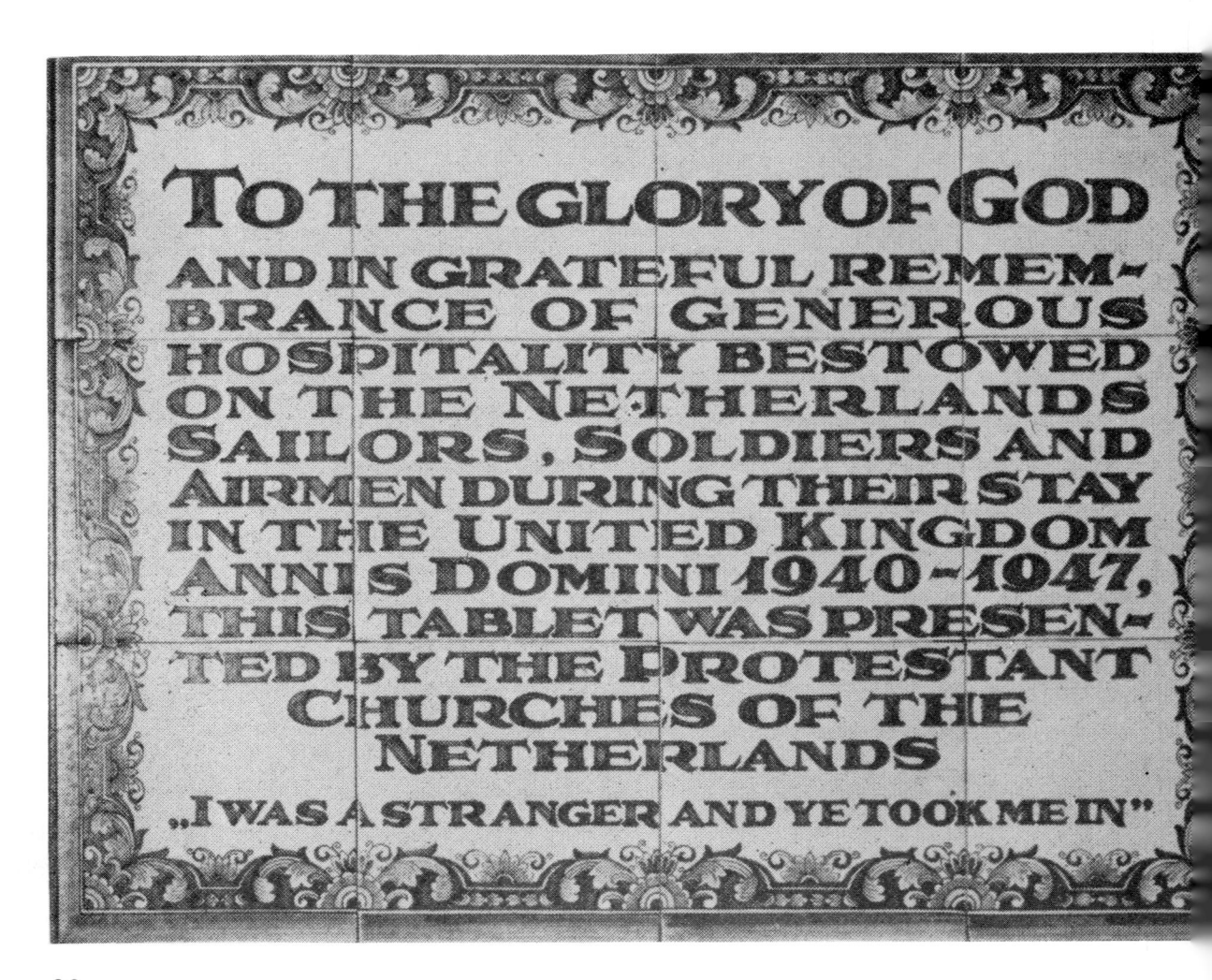

> TO THE GLORY OF GOD AND IN GRATEFUL REMEMBRANCE OF GENEROUS HOSPITALITY BESTOWED ON THE NETHERLANDS SAILORS, SOLDIERS AND AIRMEN DURING THEIR STAY IN THE UNITED KINGDOM ANNIS DOMINI 1940-1947, THIS TABLET WAS PRESENTED BY THE PROTESTANT CHURCHES OF THE NETHERLANDS
> "I WAS A STRANGER AND YE TOOK ME IN"

> His Majesty's Government is fully aware of, and much appreciates, the widespread desire of the population of the West Indian Colonies to serve in the Armed Forces . . . in particular, arrangements have been made for entry of qualified individuals into the Royal Air Force and into certain skilled trades in the Army. (*Hansard*, 8 July 1941)

ALLIED SOLDIERS IN SCOTLAND

Thomas Jones visited the University of St Andrews, Scotland, in January 1941. He found there

> a club for H.M. Forces, which is much patronised by Polish and Dutch soldiers, and when I visited it yesterday . . . a male voice choir of Poles was rehearsing with gusto. There are several thousand of them in the St. Andrews district, and scores of classes for the teaching of English are being held. (Thomas Jones, *A Diary with Letters*)

Many Polish families stayed in Britain after the war. Can you think why Poles might not want to return home? (Remember which big neighbour of Poland still had power over her, even when the Germans went: if you can't remember, look at a map.)

◀ *This inscription is in the Chapel of Remembrance at Biggin Hill Airfield, Kent. There are memorials there to Polish and Canadian pilots too.*

THE AMERICANS ARRIVE

There were mixed feelings when troops from the United States started to arrive in Britain. American soldiers, sailors and airmen were better-paid and better-clothed and fed than British troops — and most British civilians. They often had very pleasant manners and were generous with presents. Girls liked them. What does the old war-time joke, that the only things wrong with "the Yanks" were that "they were over-paid, over-sexed and over here", suggest about attitudes towards the Americans?

More friendly feelings were shown in a radio-talk by Rena Bosanquet (reported in *The Listener*, 10 September 1942), whose own children had been evacuated to the United States. She went to enquire about entertaining some American servicemen:

> We seemed to have very little to give in the way of entertainment, but the American ladies in charge of the "American Outpost" soon put me right about that. One of them said: "What these boys want is to get to know you in your homes. They don't want to be always sight-seeing and going places. What they want is to feel there is somewhere they can find a welcome"
> . . . Here are some of the things I find they really like: lots of cold water to drink with their meals, good coffee after; they like to show you places on the map, particularly their home towns and the places they have been to and above all they love to show you photographs of their people and tell you about them . . .

Can you think of any things in Britain the Americans would *not* have liked? You may be able to find out if there were any American troops stationed in your area during the war. Do you know any families who have a relation who married an American serviceman and went to the United States as a "G.I. Bride"?

Travel in War-Time

Road-travel was limited by the shortage of petrol. There was a small ration for private motorists until March 1942. Then this "basic ration" was abolished, and only essential users (like doctors) were allowed petrol for their cars. Travel for most people meant travel by train. The railways had to carry important war-materials, and they were short of staff and of coal (most trains in the 1940s were drawn by steam-engines). Passenger services were cut down. Soon, everyone had a story to tell about some dreadful train journey.

DEMAND FOR ONE-CLASS RAIL TRAVEL

It seemed to some people foolish and wrong to have compartments divided into First and Third (the equivalent of our Second) Class on crowded war-time trains. In the House of Commons in July 1941 the M.P. for Leigh put forward the case for making all trains one-class:

> "What are we fighting for? We are fighting for equality — to put everybody on the same footing. We are rationing out our food supply, so that rich and poor are

CROWDED TRAINS

From the two descriptions below, you will be able to work out the main problems facing railway-travellers. The authors, Evelyn Waugh and Anthony Powell, served as soldiers in the war. The extracts come from novels they wrote about their experiences.

> The first-class carriage was quite full, four a side, and the racks were piled high with baggage. Black funnel-shaped shields cast the light on to the passengers' laps; their faces in the surrounding darkness were indistinguishable; a naval paymaster-commander slept peacefully in one corner, two civilians strained their eyes over the evening papers; the other four were soldiers ... (Evelyn Waugh, *Put Out More Flags*)
>
> The train, long, grimy, closely packed, subject to many delays ... pushed south towards London. Within the carriages cold fug stiflingly prevailed, dimmed bulbs, just luminous .... At a halt in the Midlands, night without [*outside*] still dark as the pit, the Lancashire Fusilier next to me, who had remarked earlier he was going on leave in this neighbourhood, at once guessed the name of the totally blacked-out station, collected his kit and quitted the compartment hurriedly. His departure was welcome, even the more crowded seat now enjoying improved leg-room ...
> 'Is there a breakfast car on this train?' asked the Green Howard. '— no', said the Durham Light Infantryman. 'Where do you think you are — the Ritz?'
> One of the Signals said there was hope of a cup of tea, possibly food in some form, at the next stop, a junction where the train was alleged to remain for ten minutes or more ... (Anthony Powell, *The Valley of Bones*)

What kind of people were most of the passengers on both trains? Notice how Anthony Powell refers to his fellow-passengers: how would he know one man was in the Signals, another in the Green Howards, etc?

treated alike. Yet, on a railway journey the rich and poor must not have the same travelling facilities, unless it can be absolutely proved that there is room in the first-class compartment and no room in the third."

The Minister of War Transport replied:

"There have been, as everyone knows, instructions issued to allow first class compartments to be filled up in corridor trains when the third-class compartments are full." He would consider the matter further. (*Hansard*, 1941)

From October 1941, London suburban trains were run with third-class accommodation only.

Look back to Evelyn Waugh's description of war-time travel. What had happened to first-class compartments on that train? (Remember that there are normally three seats each side in First Class.)

Stations were so dark that it was difficult to find out where you were.

In war-time, the railway ▶ authorities tried to discourage people from travelling. Why?

1944: "D Day" and Flying-Bombs

By 1944, it was clear that the Allies were going to win the war. However, people in Britain were exhausted after such a long struggle, and it was all the harder now to bear dangers and disasters. With the invasion of Europe on "D Day" (6 June 1944) hopes rose; but the Germans had a "secret weapon".

The first pilotless plane or "flying-bomb" fell on London on 13 June 1944. These could be heard coming — then their engines cut out, there was a moment's silence, and they fell. On 8 September, the first rockets followed.

A SOUTH EAST DIARY

Mrs L. George of Bromley, Kent, kept a diary during 1944. She was a member of the A.R.P. and often on night-duty. Her diary records the good and the bad news of that summer:

Tuesday 6th June

At last it has come, Invasion Day. D. Day. I first heard the news as I was walking along Recreation Road to catch my bus to work, when a woman shot out of a doorway shouting 'It's started, they've landed troops in France'. It made me go hot and cold at first but then I couldn't help feeling very glad that it had come and we are on the last lap before peace comes. It was very exciting at the office. We listened to the news midday which was very dramatic, and in the evening we heard the King speak on the wireless.

Thursday 15th June

[A.R.P.] Post duty in evening. Warning just before twelve o'clock and what a night. Jerry sent over his jet propelled, radio-controlled-monoplane-gliders and boy, could they move. It was very exciting and we were at the post till seven in the morning.

Saturday 17th June

... I was on [duty] all night. Stayed on patrol till two fifteen. Kept diving into doorways when anything was overhead. What a night. I've never seen anything like it ... when the P.A.C's [*pilotless air-craft*] came over everything went up after them.

Monday 26th June

Mondayish day, dull and raining and plenty of Buzz Bombs going over. When I got home heard one had dropped at the Beech Tree [public house] midday and young Olive Daniels next door is missing from it ...

Olive Daniels was saved. By October 1944, the worst of the flying-bomb period was over; but now the rocket, which fell with no warning at all, appears in the diary:

Friday 20th October

There has just been a terrific explosion. One of Jerry's rockets ...

Tuesday 31st October

Nice loud bang in the middle of the night. They are getting quite frequent lately ...

Mrs George wrote up her memories of the war, based on her diary, when she was an old lady, and gave her local library a copy.

LEARNING TO LIVE WITH THE FLYING-BOMBS

Notice the different names given to the flying-bombs: why do you think they were soon nicknamed "Buzz Bombs"? (Another nickname for them was "doodle-bugs".)

You'll find another name for them in the following advertisement, inserted in local papers on 29 June 1944:

> ROBOT PLANES!
> We are pleased to be in a position to announce that we have an Air Raid Shelter which can accommodate 1,500 people below our new building . . .
> GRANTS BROS. LTD. CROYDON

George Orwell, the author, has left a good description of what it was like to live in the flying-bomb area:

After the wail of the siren comes the zoom-zoom-zoom of the bomb, and as it draws nearer you get up from your table and squeeze yourself into some corner that flying glass is not likely to reach. Then BOOM! the windows rattle in their sockets and you go back to work.

Everyone's first thought was that the bang meant the bomb had missed *them*. The next thought was for the people who had been hit. It was particularly nasty being at school during the day, sitting in the cellars or shelters and wondering if the bomb had dropped on your home.

People hated the flying-bombs more than the rockets; why, do you think?

HEAVY DAMAGE

The flying-bombs and rockets caused much damage and many casualties (6,184 people were killed by the bombs and 2,754 by rockets). You can see where most of them fell from the list below:

> Thursday, September 14th, 1944
> *Beckenham and Penge Advertiser*
> WORST HIT BOROUGHS
> The 13 worst-blitzed boroughs all lie to the South and East [of London]. Here they are in order, according to the official list.

Croydon
Wandsworth
Lewisham
Camberwell
Woolwich
Greenwich
Beckenham

Lambeth
Orpington
Coulsdon & Purley
West Ham
Chislehurst
Mitcham

Luckily, allied forces in Europe soon captured most launching sites for these weapons. The last fell on Britain in March 1945.

Amusements and Celebration

By modern standards, war-time amusements were simple. An evening out at a cinema or a dance-hall was the height of excitement for most people. Everyone longed for the end of the war, when they felt they would really be able to enjoy themselves. As a popular song of 1943 put it, "I'm Gonna Get Lit Up When the Lights Go Up in London..."

PLACES TO GO

You could find your evening's entertainment from advertisements like these in the local newspaper. (Beckenham is a South London suburb.)

DANCING EVERY FRIDAY
7.30-11 p.m. (closed Good Friday)
REGAL BALLROOM, BECKENHAM
RHYTHM SWING BAND

Admission	Cash
1/6	Spot
Forces	Prizes
1/-	

Regal Cinema Beckenham
Friday & Saturday	Little Nellie Kelly
	So You Won't Talk
Sunday	Remember
	Escape to Paradise
Next week	Angels over Broadway
	A Modern Hero

(*Beckenham & Penge Advertiser*, April 1941)

Notice the time the dances end (why did people need to get home early?) and the reduced prices for people in the armed forces. Cinema goers at this time expected value-for-money — two long films in each programme.

Books were much in demand, but paper shortages led to restrictions. If you see old books printed on thin, poor paper, look inside at the front: you may find a statement that they conform to "authorized economy standards". Newspapers and magazines were smaller too, with fewer pages. Notice the "Utility" symbol.

This advertisement is a reminder of the importance of radio during the war. Television had only recently been developed, and was shut down at the out-break of war. For most families, radio was the chief form of entertainment. "It's that man again" was a catch-phrase everyone would have known. The initials (I.T.M.A.) formed the name of a popular comedy show whose star, Tommy Handley, was "that man".

"It's that man again..."

Your Ferranti set is certainly five years old — maybe twelve. It has probably given you thousands of hours service but even the best set built will not live for ever. Should your set require overhaul our dealers and ourselves will do all we can help you. And that applies Ferranti Electric Clocks a Fires too.

FERRANTI rad
ELECTRIC CLOCKS and FI
Ferranti Ltd 36 Kingsway London

BOOKS IN BATTLEDRESS

"INK," SAID VISCOUNT SAMUEL, in a famous debate on book production, "can do nothing without its colleague, paper." The publisher's paper ration is only 40% of his pre-war consumption, yet the demand for books of all kinds has never been so great.

Therefore, books are in battledress, and the book you buy to-day has narrower margins (*equals more words to the page*) thinner paper (*paper is reckoned by weight*) and lighter binding. Even then, the demand exceeds the supply.

Don't grumble because the particular book you want is unobtainable, nor argue that it should take precedence of another book that somebody else wants just as much. The publisher must try to cater for all tastes.

Please do not hold up the exchange of your Book Token because a particular book is out of stock. A book in the hand is worth two in the press!

Britain Needs Books by John Brophy explains the difficulties of wartime book production. Obtainable at all good bookshops 1/3 net

Book Tokens Ltd.

"V.E. DAY"

By spring 1945, the biggest celebration of all was in sight. Already on 18 April the council of Bromley, Kent, was making plans for "the day when the end of the war in Europe is announced". They decided:

> 1. On V.E. Day, the clergy would hold Thanksgiving Services in their own Churches.
> 2. On the following day at 11 a.m. a public Thanksgiving Service would be held on the Queens Mead [a local open space] ... and during the evening ... music would be provided for dancing and singing ...
>
> (Bromley Council Minutes, 18 April 1945)

"V.E. Day" finally came on Tuesday 8 May, but the public did not wait for official celebrations:

> Penge, in common with many districts in and around London, started the celebration of victory on Monday night .... Not much happened till night-fall. Then bonfires which had been hastily prepared on bombed sites ... began to appear, and in the light they cast people sang and danced among skeleton walls, to accordion and other music, till well past midnight ...
>
> Another victory note was that sounded by the drivers of steam trains with a hearty chorus of whistle blasts ... The main celebrations, of course, were reserved for V.E. Day itself. Tuesday, in very truth, provided a night of nights. Dancing, singing and revelry in the streets went on half-way through the night ...
>
> (*Beckenham and Penge Advertiser*, Thursday, 10 May, 1945)

CHANGING CUSTOMS

Women began to go out by themselves more, and to places which before the war had been visited chiefly by men. The Welsh girl whose experiences at work in a Labour Exchange are described on page 24 remembers:

> ... we looked around for ways in which to spend our hard earned money. And women invaded the pubs. Locally, at least, they had never done so pre-war. But they were by no means always welcome. Indeed three (myself included) were refused a drink at a smart Newport hotel because we were "unaccompanied" [by a man] ...

See what else you can find out about V.E. celebrations, in your own area or elsewhere. Many Londoners went up to cheer the King and Queen at Buckingham Palace: perhaps you can discover someone who celebrated in this way. Find out too how "V.J. Day" (when the war with Japan ended) was celebrated.

Date List

3 September 1939	War begins.
10 May 1940	Germany invades Holland and Belgium. Churchill replaces Chamberlain as Prime Minister and forms a National Government (with Liberal and Labour members as well as Conservatives).
3-4 June 1940	British troops are evacuated from Dunkirk. It was lucky for Britain that these troops were not captured by the Germans. If they had been, few trained soldiers would have remained to defend Britain from invasion.
11 June 1940	Italy joins in the war as Germany's ally.
22 June 1940	France surrenders to Germany.
1 July 1940	Germany occupies the Channel Islands.
13 August-15 September 1940	The R.A.F. wins the "Battle of Britain".
September 1940	The bombing of British cities — the "Blitz" — begins.
22 June 1941	Germany attacks Russia. Britain and Russia are now allies.
7 December 1941	Japan attacks the U.S. fleet at Pearl Harbour. The United States becomes an ally of Britain and Russia against both Germany and Japan.
15 February 1942	The Japanese capture Singapore from Britain.
October-November 1942	In North Africa, Britain wins the battle of El Alamein. British and American troops land in French North Africa (Algeria and Morocco).
December 1942	At home, the Beveridge Report on the social services (with plans for reform) is presented.
July 1943	Allied troops land in Sicily.
September 1943	Allied troops invade Italy.
6 June 1944	"D Day" — Allied troops invade France.
13 June 1944	First "flying-bomb" falls on Britain.
8 September 1944	First German rocket falls on Britain.
8 May 1945	"VE Day — war ends in Europe.
14 August 1945	Japan asks for peace after atom bombs are dropped on Hiroshima and Nagasaki.
2 September 1945	"VJ Day" (official).

Difficult Words

A.R.P.	Air-Raid Precautions. Also used for the wardens, who enforced regulations and helped people during raids.
A.T.S.	Auxiliary Territorial Service — the women's section of the army.
barracks	living-quarters for those in the armed forces.
barrage balloon	large balloon, tethered by ropes, intended to prevent enemy aircraft from flying low.
battalion	army unit, usually of about 1,000 soldiers.
Bevin Boy	young man sent to work in the mines instead of serving in the armed forces. (As Minister of Labour, Ernest Bevin was responsible for this scheme.)
black-out	the elimination, as far as possible, of all lights that might be seen from the air. Houses had to have all windows covered after dark.
"Blitz"	a shortened version of the German word "Blitzkreig" which means "lightning war". The British used it to describe constant heavy bombing raids.
buzz-bomb	German V1 or "flying-bomb", a pilotless aeroplane carrying a bomb.
camouflage	a disguise for military equipment (for example, nets with leaves stuck into them).
censorship	control by the government of news and information.
"civvy-street"	service slang for "civilian life".
coupons	part of the rationing system; small squares of paper were cut out of the ration book when a purchase was made.
duration, the	the length of time the war lasted.
egg-powder	dried egg (water had to be added to make it up).
embarkation	soldiers "embarked" on ships to go overseas; they were given a short period of leave (embarkation leave) to say good-bye to their families before they left Britain.
evacuees	people sent from a dangerous area to an area thought to be safe.
G.I.	United States soldier. A girl who married an American serviceman was called a "G.I. bride".
Home Guard	British part-time volunteer force, for home defence.
incendiary	a small bomb designed to start fires.
mines	floating bombs which exploded when a ship knocked against them. (There were also "land-mines" dropped from the air — a kind of bomb.)
N.C.O.	a Non-Commissioned Officer (e.g. a Sergeant).
Nissen hut	a temporary building, of corrugated iron on a concrete base.
pill-box	a small fort; part of the anti-invasion defences.
R.A.O.C.	Royal Army Ordnance Corps. The R.A.O.C. looked after military stores and equipment.
rationing	sharing out equally scarce food and materials.
Red Cross	the International organization which helps people in need. In war-time, this includes prisoners-of-war, people in occupied countries, etc.
refugee	someone obliged to leave his or her own country to escape ill-treatment.
salvage	waste materials that could be useful to the war-effort.
squander-bug	an imaginary creature used in National Savings advertisements. It "worked for Hitler" by trying to get people to "squander" money, i.e. to spend instead of saving.
time-bomb	a bomb set to go off at a certain time, instead of exploding at once.
war-artists	a group of artists employed by the government to make a pictorial record of the war.

Places to Visit

Imperial War Museum, Lambeth Road, London.
Museum of London, London Wall, London.
Watford Museum, 194, High Street, Watford, Herts.
(These museums all have good displays showing what life was like for civilians in the Second World War.)

You can see aircraft from the Second World War at:
Biggin Hill Airfield, Kent.
Birmingham Museum of Science and Industry.
Duxford Airfield, Cambridgeshire (an extension of the Imperial War Museum).
R.A.F. Museum, Hendon

Churchill's underground headquarters in London — the Cabinet War Rooms, Whitehall — are now open to the public. You can see them exactly as they were left when the war ended.

This display is in Watford Museum. Notice the map showing where bombs fell and the member of the Home Guard (with military gas-mask). A pack of material on war-time life, produced by the Museum and local teachers, can be borrowed by local schools.

Book List

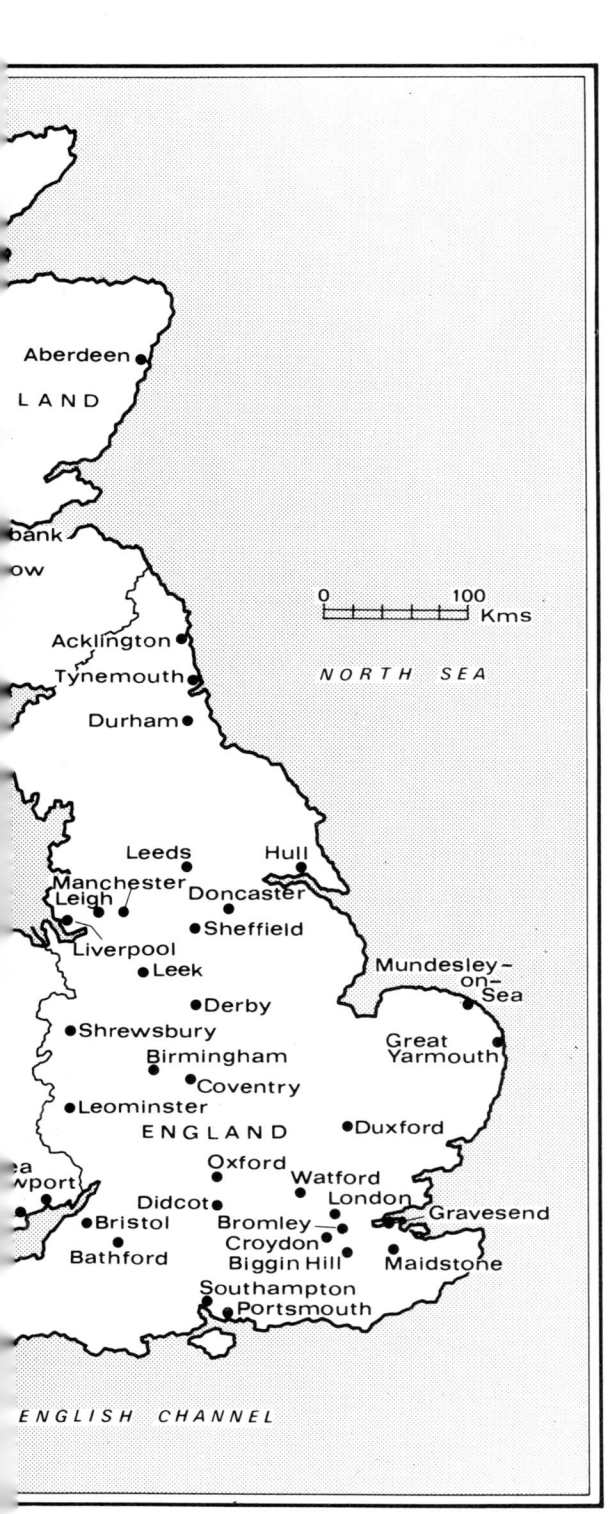

Books for Younger Readers
Fox, Edward, *The Battle of Britain*, Lutterworth (When and Why series), 1969
Fyson, Nance Lui, *Growing Up in the Second World War*, Batsford (Growing Up series), 1981

Books for Older Readers
There are many books about life in war-time Britain. Large reference books like Basil Collier's *The Defence of the United Kingdom*, HMSO, 1957, are packed with interesting details. For local information, there is R. Douglas Brown's series, *East Anglia 1939, 1940* etc, published by Terence Dalton, Lavenham, and the "Action Station" series and "Aviation Enthusiasts' Guides" published by Patrick Stephens, Cambridge (these give details of war-time airfields, and the "Guides" describe some bombing incidents too). Published Diaries like those used in this book — Harold Nicolson's, Thomas Jones', for example — are available in libraries, as are the other books listed below, which are particularly useful:

Calder, Angus, *The People's War*, Cape, 1969
Chamberlin, E.R., *Life in Wartime Britain*, Batsford, 1972
Harrison, Tom, *Living Through the Blitz*, Collins, 1976
Jones, Thomas, *A Diary with Letters 1931-1950*, O.U.P., 1954
Longmate, Norman, *How We Lived Then*, Hutchinson, 1971
Longmate, Norman (editor) *The Home Front*, Chatto & Windus, 1981
Minns, Raynes, *Bombers & Mash: the Domestic Front 1939-45*, Virago, 1980
Nicolson, Harold, *Diaries and Letters, 1939-1945*, ed. Nigel Nicolson, Collins, 1967

There is a valuable section on school-life in the 1939-45 war in Denis Tye's *A Village School: Boughton Monchelsea 1850-1970*, published by Prototype, Sittingbourne, Kent, and obtainable from D. Tye at Boughton Monchelsea C.P. School, Nr Maidstone, Kent.

Index

Acklington 12
advertisements 9, 15, 33, 42
air-raids 8, 10, 14-17, 19, 25, 40-41
allies 36-37
Americans 36-37
army, life in 22-23
A.R.P. 9, 40, 45
atom-bomb 44
A.T.S. 5, 22, 30, 45
Avonmouth 15

barrage-balloons 7, 45
Battle of Britain 12, 44
Bevin boys 4, 44
Bevin, Ernest, Minister of Labour 24, 44
Biggin Hill 12, 37
Birmingham 14, 15, 16-17
blackout 7, 8-9, 28, 38-39, 44
Blitz 14-17, 44, 45
Bristol 15, 21
Bromley, Kent 40, 43

canteens 18, 25, 27
Cardiff 15, 17
casualties 3, 5, 14, 17, 41
censorship 28
Chamberlain, Neville 7, 44
children 8
　clothes for 11, 32, 33
　evacuation of 6, 7, 8, 10-11, 13
　at school 18-19
　war-work 26
Chislehurst 3, 9, 16, 41
Churchill, Winston 13, 44
cinemas 41
clothes 11
　rationing of 32-33
　women's 20, 22, 33
Clydebank 3
Commons, House of 7, 8, 32, 36-37, 38-39
conscription 6
Cooper, Duff 7
Croydon 9, 33, 41

dances 42
D Day 40, 44
Derby 15
Didcot 22, 30
Doncaster 4
dried egg 30, 45
Dunkirk 12, 30, 44
Durham 18

Eden, Anthony 12
Elizabeth, Princess 3

embarkation leave 34-35, 45
evacuees 6, 7, 8, 10-11, 13

factories 24-25
flying-bombs 19, 28, 40-41, 45
food, rationing of 30-31
France, fall of 12, 44
　landings in 40, 44

gas-masks 13, 46
George VI, King 3, 17, 43
Gravesend 7, 10
Great Yarmouth 7, 10

hairstyles, women's 24-25
Handley, Tommy 42
Home Guard 12-13, 46
Hull 15
Huxley, Julian 6

incendiary bombs 3, 45
industry 24-25, 32
invasion precautions 12-13

Jamaica 36
Jones, Thomas 14, 37

Keyes, Sidney 21

Land Army 33
Leeds 13
Leominster 35
Lewis, Alun 23
Liverpool 15, 16-17
London 5, 7
　bombing of 14-16
　schools in 18-19
　university of 20-21
　zoo 6

Macmillan, Harold 7
Maidstone 7
Malta 29
Manchester 15
Merchant Navy 34-35
Ministry of Food 30-31
Ministry of Information 27
museums 5, 46

National Savings 27, 29
Newport, Gwent 35, 43
Nicolson, Harold 7
Norfolk 8, 10, 13

Orwell, George 28, 41
Oxford 7, 20, 21, 30, 35

pill-box 4, 5
poetry 21, 23, 31
Poland, Poles 3, 36-37
Portsmouth 15
posters 24, 39
Powell, Anthony 38
prisoners of war 34-35
propaganda 28-29

radio 28, 40, 42
rationing 38
　clothes 32-33
　food 30-31
　petrol 38
recipes 30-31
rockets 40-41

St Andrews 37
salvage 26-27
sand-bags 7
schools, schoolchildren 18-19
Sheffield 15
shelters 8, 14-15, 16
shops 9, 32-33, 41
Shrewsbury 16-17
songs 34, 42
Sorrell, Alan 6
Southampton 15
Spender, Stephen 3
Swansea 15

trains 38-39
travel 13, 38-39
trenches 9
Tynemouth 18

uniform, school 18-19
universities 20-21
"Utility" 32, 43

victory celebrations 43
VE Day 43, 44
VJ Day 43, 44

war-artists 5, 23
war, declaration of 7
war-work 24-25
Waugh, Evelyn 38
Weight, Carel 23
Weissenborn, Helmuth 14, 16
West Indians 36-37
Woolf, Virginia 30
W.V.S. 27

zoo, London 6

319755   6.95

SIR HENRY COOPER HIGH SCHOOL
LIBRARY